P9-BBP-094

# VACATION

# VACATION

## We're Going to the Ocean



POEMS BY

David L. Harrison

ILLUSTRATIONS BY

Rob Shepperson

WORDSONG

*Honesdale, Pennsylvania*

Printed in China
Designed by Helen Robinson
First edition

Library of Congress Cataloging-in-Publication Data

Harrison, David L. (David Lee).
Vacation : we're going to the ocean : poems / by David Harrison ; drawings by Rob Shepperson. — 1st ed.
p. cm.
ISBN 978-1-59078-568-3 (hardcover : alk. paper)
1. Family recreation—Juvenile poetry. 2. Ocean—Juvenile poetry.
3. Vacations—Juvenile poetry. 4. Children's poetry, American.
I. Shepperson, Rob, ill. II. Title.
PS3558.A6657V33 2008
811'.54—dc22
2008017718

**WORDSONG**
An Imprint of Boyds Mills Press, Inc.
815 Church Street
Honesdale, Pennsylvania 18431

*To Allen and Elinor Burstein,*
*our friends by the sea*
—D.L.H.

*For Tessa*
—R.S.

## Contents

Contents

## Hi!



Call me
Sam,
that's who
I am.

Samuel
I'm not,

except
when
I'm in
trouble,

I'm
"Sam-u-el Scott!"

When
my sister
has a snit,

I'm
"You
big
snot!"

Mostly,
though,
I'm
just
plain
Sam.

# We're Going to the Ocean!

Man oh
man oh
man oh
man,
we're going
to the
ocean!

I'm going to see
sharks
and whales!

I'm going to see
pirate sails!

I'm going to see
fish that glow!

Man oh
man oh
man,
let's go!

## In the Backseat



We're taking
a trip!

We're taking
the car!

We're going
to places
way,
way
far!

Taking a trip
will be
so neat,

especially
in the
backseat.

## Packing

My gerbil
can't go,

but
I need
a pet.

My parents
don't know
of my
spider
yet.

## Loading the Car



My sister
packed
so much
junk

there's
no place
I can sit.

If we
left
my sister
home,

I bet
her stuff
would
fit.

# Are We There Yet?

My foot's
asleep,

my seat
is sore.

You said
"another hour"
before.

You say
"an hour"
every
time.

Your
hours
are much

longer
than
mine.

# Pass the Wieners

Mommy said,
"Turn left."

Daddy
turned
right.

Now
we're
somewhere—

out
of
gas—

camping
for
the
night.

## At the Art Museum



Don't like
pictures
like
that.

They need
some
clothes

or a
hat.

## Out the Window

Look!

A tiger!

A crouching
tiger
with black
stripes
and yellow
hair!

No?

You sure?

Look!

A bear!

# I Gotta Go!



Oh!

Oh!

Oh!

Oh!

Stop the car!
I gotta go!

Stop the car
before
I pop!

Please!

Please!

Please!

Stop!

# Spending the Night with Relatives

Every time
we spend
the night,

our cousins
start
a bedtime
fight.

Cousins
never
get caught.

This is
lots of fun—
not!

# Aunty Hugs



Uncles mess
your
hair,

shake
your
hand—

things
guys
understand.

Aunties
grab you

in a
hug
attack.

You gotta
hug them
back.

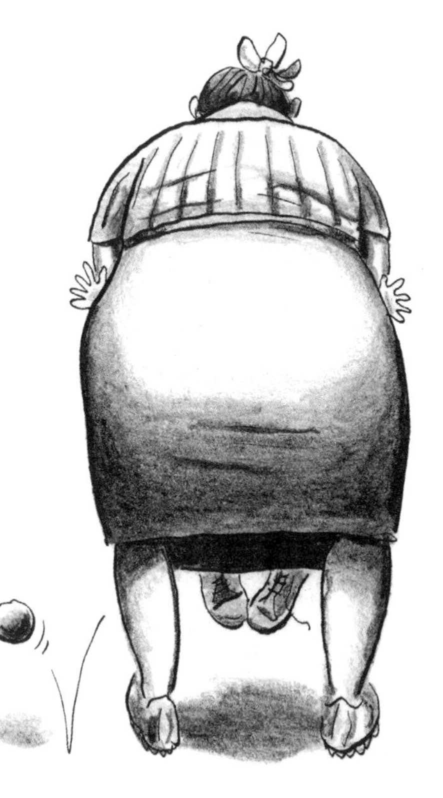

# Oops!

Hold
my
spider?

He
won't
mind—

oops!

He
may be
hard
to
find.

## Beside the Road



He wouldn't
crawl
far.

I hope
he's in
the car.

Why
did you
have to
shout?

I bet
you
let
him
out!

## Fast Food

(FOR TWO VOICES)

"I want a
jumbo
burger."

"No."

"I want an
order of
fries."

"No."

"I want a
chocolate
shake."

"No."

I know why
they call this
fast food.

There's
always
*"No"*
waiting.

ear in Provence

## Uck! Ick!

Open a window!

Give me air!

The baby pooted!

It's not fair!

I'll gag to death!

Good-bye!

I'm doomed!

Uck!

Ick!

I'm baby-fumed!

# Hiking



What a
cool
place
to hike.

I see tons
of stuff
I like.

Wish
I had
a bigger
jar.

I'd take
these
scorpions
in
the
car.

# Motel Pool

Look
out!

Belly
whopper!

When Sister
starts,

it's hard to
stop her!

## Ice Machine

We filled
the tub
with
ice cubes,

and Mommy
got
upset.

We thought
it would be
funny,
but

the floor
got sort of
wet.

## Sleeping Daddy

Daddy's
snoring
sounds
like drains
gurgling,

doors
squeaking,

monsters
roaring!

No one ever
gets to
sleep

when
Daddy's
snoring.

## Putting Up the Tent



We
helped
Daddy
with the
tent.

It didn't
go
the way
we meant.

We don't
know how
the pole
got bent.

## Campground Showers

I'm teasing
Daddy.

We're
having
fun.

That's not
Daddy.

Help!
Run!

# What Was That?

(FOR TWO VOICES)

<table>
<tr><td>Pssst!</td><td></td></tr>
<tr><td></td><td>Listen!</td></tr>
<tr><td>What was</td><td></td></tr>
<tr><td></td><td>that?</td></tr>
<tr><td>A monster</td><td></td></tr>
<tr><td></td><td>quiet as a</td></tr>
<tr><td>cat</td><td></td></tr>
<tr><td></td><td>with one<br>bright eye</td></tr>
<tr><td>and<br>Daddy's<br>grin.</td><td></td></tr>
<tr><td></td><td>Zip the<br>flap!</td></tr>
<tr><td>Don't<br>let him in!</td><td></td></tr>
</table>

# Rainy Day

Grown-ups
stay inside
and fret.

Kids
don't care
if they
get wet.

It's a
squishy,
splashy
day.

Come on,
everybody!

Play!

# Horseback



When I say
"Go!"
she doesn't.

When I say
"Whoa!"
she won't.

My horse
may think
I like her ...

I don't.

# Rattlesnake Country

A rattlesnake
A rattlesnake
I wanna see a rattlesnake
I wanna see a rattlesnake
I wanna see a—

Hey!

Was that a rattle?

Hang onto your saddle!

# Tarantula



Help me
take him
home
with me.

Sister,
why'd
you
climb
that
tree?

# The Ocean!

(FOR TWO VOICES)

(Sam) (Sister)

Daddy!
Daddy!
It's the
ocean!
Wow!
It's great!

See
the ocean?
See
the beaches?
See
the shore?

I want
to get
in the
water
now!
I can't
wait!

Daddy!
Daddy!
Hurry!
What
are we
waiting for?

## Shark!

Shark!

Shark!

Shark
in the bay!

Never mind,
it flew away.

# Hot Pop

It's cool
shaking
hot pop
and
spewing it!

Not fair
getting
time out
for
doing it.

## Taking Pictures

I caught
Daddy
busy
cooking

and Sister
when
she
wasn't
looking

but
these
gulls
won't
hold
steady.
I'm nearly
out
of
pictures
already!

## The Beach

Daddy
helped us
bury
Mommy,

Mommy
helped us
bury
Sister,

Sister
helped us
bury
Daddy.

Oh-oh!
I better go.

## Brother's Turn



Maybe Sister
had a hand

in filling
Brother's
shorts
with
sand.

All I know is,

he
can't
stand.

# No-see-ums

No-see-ums
are hard
to see.

I looked
for them,

but they
found me.

## Sunburn

Mommy says
we have
to learn
to keep
our skin
from getting
burned.

She lathers on
enough
lotion
to leave rings
around
the ocean.

# Swimsuits

People
don't care

what
you
see.

That suit
would be

too
small

on
me.

# Fishing

Hey, mister!

Mister?

Mister?

Need some bait?

Take my sister!

# Snorkeling



Guess
what
I saw
down
there!

A bony
fish
with
funny
hair!

Oh,
well,
silly
me.

It
was
only
Daddy's
knee.

## Our Sand Castle

Sister and I
worked hours
on that,

then Brother
comes
and knocks
it flat.

## Shopping



Sister needs swim fins,
Daddy needs vitamins,

Brother needs a sun cap,
Daddy needs a road map,

Mommy needs lotion,
I NEED THE OCEAN!

## Iguana

Is that a lizard
or an alligator?

If it moves this way,
I'll see you later!

## Souvenir



My tennis shoe's
the perfect
size

to hold
my little
secret
prize.

I can't wait
to see
their
eyes

when
they meet
my crab
surprise.

# Going Home

I'm glad I'm not
too big
for Mommy's lap.

I don't know
if I should,
but, boy,
does it feel good,

and it's
the perfect place
to take a nap.

# Beside the Road Again

Yuck!
The crab
inside my
shoe!

Unfortunately,

it died there.

Phew!

## Home at Last!

Group hug.

Our trip was neat,
especially
in the backseat.

Everything we did was fun.
Group hug for everyone!

Home at last!
I'm glad we're here,

but I can't wait
until next year!